DREAM: UNRAVEL ITS MYSTERIES

By
Alexander O. Sign

Published by New Generation Publishing in 2013

Copyright © Alexander O. Sign 2013

First Edition

The author asserts the moral right under the Copyright, Designs and Patents Act 1988 to be identified as the author of this work.

All Rights reserved. No part of this publication may be reproduced, stored in a retrieval system or transmitted, in any form or by any means without the prior consent of the author, nor be otherwise circulated in any form of binding or cover other than that which it is published and without a similar condition being imposed on the subsequent purchaser.

www.newgeneration-publishing.com

 **New Generation Publishing**

Unless otherwise indicated, Scripture quotations are taken from The Holy Bible, New International Version. Copyright © 1973, 1978, 1984 by International Bible Society. Used by permission of International Bible Society.

References noted as HCSB are from the Holman Christian Standard Bible. Copyright © 1999, 2000, 2002, 2003 by Holman Bible Publishers. Used by permission.

References noted as KJV are from the King James Version. Copyright © 1994 by Thomas Nelson, Inc. All rights reserved. Used by permission.

References noted as NASB are from the New American Standard Bible. Copyright © 1960, 1962, 1963, 1968, 1971, 1972, 1973, 1975, 1977, 1995 by The Lockman Foundation. Used by permission.

Contact:
For questions, inquiry, prayer and the purchase of additional copies of this book and other books written by this author, write or call:
E-mail: glospelnetry@live.com, alexandersign07@gmail.com
Tel: +23408131274996, +23407057236992

To
Late Chief Sign Emeranewune Orereh
my beloved father who was gifted with the
understanding of dreams

Acknowledgements

Dream is a life long exposure and experience that I am personally grateful for to God. To experience dream and unravel its mysteries is a rare privilege that makes one marvel at God and His unfathomable wisdom. I'm grateful to God for dreams and for the individuals He used in inspiring this great adventure in me.

My humble and heartfelt appreciation goes to my dear and beloved father Chief Sign Emeranewune Orereh who gratefully shared most of his dreams with me. He inspired the quest to unravel dream's mysteries in me. The importance and place I have accorded dream in my personal walk with God stems from him and the biblical teachings on dream. The actual occurrence and fulfillment of most of his dreams and his interpretations of them drove the message home in me: *"Dream is a medium of divine revelation."* Daddy, this book is a perpetual remembrance of you in my life. I can hardly forget you.

I am grateful to all the members of Global Gospel Network Ministry for their unfeigning support. My appreciation to Dan Oteri and his children: Ese and Oghenero Oteri, Pastor Rosemary Achioyamen, Timothy Okiki and Pastor Mike and Pastor (Mrs.) Monica Okosodo for their numerous encouragements during the writing of this book. You are wonderful people. And to Pastor Blessing Ogagaoghene who proofread the manuscript and the entire family of Mr. Christopher and Mrs. Theresa Oraekwugha who graciously made their home ours. We always feel at home with them. You are unique people, rare gems. We deeply love you. God Bless you.

My love goes to my dearest and beloved wife, Pastor (Mrs.) Treasure M. Reeves Sign and our children - Miss Hesed Oghenetega Sign and Master Jedidiah Ovie Sign for their continuous support and encouragement. Your sacrificial lives made this book a reality. God richly bless you. I love you all.

All thanks and praises to Jesus, the great mystery of godliness made manifest in the flesh and to God Almighty the giver of all truth, wisdom, knowledge and understanding, and the revealer of all mysteries. Amen.

Alexander Otovwe Sign
Effurun, Delta State
May, 2013.

Contents

Acknowledgements 7

Introduction 11

1. Biblical Teachings on Dreams 1 19

2. Biblical Teachings on Dreams II 29

3. How to tackle Dreams 43

4. Biblical Truths That Dreams Reaffirm 58

Conclusion 68

Introduction

There is hardly an experience, apart from sleep, that is common to humanity like dream. There is hardly a person under the sun that has not dreamt at one time or the other. The experience of dream cuts across geographical locations, climatic differences, religious, racial, national and sexual discriminations. All persons of all religions, races, nationalities, ethnicities and sexes have at one time or another dreamed. It also cuts across all social and financial status of life: kings as well as subjects (servants), the rich as well as the poor, leaders as well as the led (followers), married as well as singles, the educated as well as the uneducated, the privileged as well as the less privileged, the religious as well as the irreligious; all classes of people dream at one time or the other. Everyone dreams.

Dream, though a common experience among humans, assumes various forms in terms of its kind, duration, visibility and its impression and impact on people's lives. Someone might experience blissfulness in a dream. Another might experience terror. Still another might experience bizarreness in a dream. Sometimes, a person might experience a blend of blissfulness, terror and bizarreness in a life time or even in a night or in just a dream. Some, depending on the nature of their dream, might wake up hopeful and cheerful; while some others might awake in terror and dread, completely paralyzed by fears. Still others might awake confused, with their minds blank, not even with the slightest clue of what they dreamt or as if they never had a dream. These persons might be conscious that they dreamed but what exactly, they know not. Some just awake as if they never dreamed or if there is any such consciousness, as long as they can't lay hands on it, they just cast it into the sea of oblivion. Everyone dreams, but not everyone recalls.

Dream, as common as it is, is one experience that some persons seldom comprehend. Its commonness has most times bewildered people's natural senses and abilities. The educated as well as the uneducated have, at one time or the other, been puzzled as to the meaning or interpretation of a dream. Science is yet to furnish the world with reasons (whether speculated or authenticated) why some people experience frequent dreams than others, and why people of different religious, racial, national and social backgrounds can attempt the interpretation of dreams, while others are totally ignorant. Everyone dreams, but not everyone interprets.

The importance one attaches to dreams spring from a person's family, religious, and societal background. One's experience of the physical occurrence of what has been dreamed, especially preciseness in the unfolding of events in a person's life, whether in the immediate or distant future, can also make a person attach importance to dreams. Notwithstanding the significance a person attaches to dreams, the indisputable reality of dreams is, some do come true, some can be averted, while others hardly happen in real life. But the mystery that still trails humanity is, who can tell which dream(s) will come true or can be averted or will never happen? Not every dream comes true.

The term "dream" has several meanings and can be used in several ways. Dream can be used in reference to a person's vision, goal, aspiration and pursuit for life. For instance, John's dream is to become an engineer or a pilot. The term "dream" can also be used to mean a person's desire and expectation. For instance, "My dream is to have Grace as a wife." "There goes my dream car." These are statements that convey a person's desire and expectation. None of these usages are in view in my discourse on dream.

In this book, the word "dream" is restrictively used to describe a person's experience during sleep. This sleep is not only during the night hours but whenever and wherever a person sleeps.

What is a Dream?

According to the *Webster's Ninth New Collegiate Dictionary*, a dream is a series of thoughts, images, or emotions occurring during sleep; it is a visionary creation of the imagination. This definition shows dream to be solely the work of the human's mind, imagination or emotion. It is the creation of the human's mind or imagination. This means dream is purely human and this cannot be expected to have any impart beyond the individual's sleep. Scientists and humanists will naturally accept this position and declare it true. But I want to challenge your perception and understanding of dream by the following questions:

1. Why do some people awake from dream(s) hopeful and reassured, and some others awake screaming, trembling and frightened?

2. Why do some people look for meaning or interpretation to certain dream(s)?

3. Why do medical doctors and psychiatrists administer tranquilizers and other drugs as they deem necessary to persons who suffer from continuous and traumatic nightmares?

4. Why do some dreams come true and others averted when properly tackled?

5. Why do some people suffer from dream phobia?

In addition to these questions, whoever had at one time or another dreamed and experienced the actual occurrence of a dream, and also witnessed or heard testimonies of people of any walk of life attesting to a dream come true, knows dream goes beyond our human's mind or imagination. To everyone who is a Christian, the experience of dream finds true meaning and importance as one goes through the pages of Scripture.

The Scripture records men who dreamt and actually saw their dreams come true. It also records teachings on the subject of dream that shed greater light on dream than any other book in the entire universe. These teachings, when correctly applied, guarantee a sure victory to every believer in the Lord Jesus.

In Genesis 41:25,28 and Daniel 2:28, two ancient monarchs had dreams and each sought for the interpretation of their dreams. Joseph nicknamed a dreamer (Genesis 37:19) and Daniel, a man gifted with understanding dreams and visions (Daniel 1:17; 5:12), interpreted these dreams. Both dreams and interpretations came true. In their discourse, they made the following statements that will enable us define dream biblically:

> *Then Joseph said to Pharaoh, "The dreams of Pharaoh are one and the same. **God has revealed to Pharaoh what he is about to do**.*
> *"It is just as I said to Pharaoh: God has shown Pharaoh what he is about to do.*
> **Genesis 41:25,28, emphasis mine**

*but there is a God in heaven who reveals mysteries. He has show King Nebuchadnezzar **what will happen in days to come.** Your dream and the visions that passed through your mind as you lay on your bed are these:*
Daniel 2:28, emphasis mine.

From these Scriptures, a dream could be defined as a revelation of what God is about to do either in the near or distant future to a person (that is, the dreamer). This revelation is not the imagination or creation of the dreamer's mind or emotion, but one communicated to the dreamer's mind by God. This is one prominent means or medium God uses in speaking to people over the globe, but unfortunately most people, being spiritually blind, are ignorant. Job 33:14-16 affirms this when it declares, "For God does speak – now one way, now another – though man may not perceive it. In a dream, in a vision of the night, when deep sleep falls on men as they slumber in their beds, he may speak in their ears and terrify them with warnings." Only this can account for the universality of dreams among all humans. Remember, everyone dreams.

Dream is a special means designed by God to speak to His people, especially His servants. The Lord's own speech to Moses, Aaron and Miriam affirms it. The Lord Himself declares; *"'when a prophet of the LORD is among you, I reveal myself to him in visions, **I speak to him in dreams**'"* (Numbers 12:6, emphasis mine). But unfortunately, some of His servants like Saul seldom hear from God in their dreams (1 Samuel 28:6,15). In the New Testament, dream is one of the Holy Spirit packages to Christians. In Acts 2:17, Peter, quoting Joel's Prophecy, declared, *"In the last days, God says, I will pour out my Spirit on all people. Your* *sons and daughters will prophesy ... see visions ... **dream dreams***" (cf Joel 2:28, emphasis mine). Thus, Christians ought to see dreams in significantly different light than non-Christians. Dream is not a human invention. It is God's designed means or medium of revelation to His people. In your dreams discern God's message. In your dreams unravel God's mysteries.

Repeated Dreams

Dreams are sometimes repeated. In some cases, this repetition takes place in one night like Pharaoh's. The Scripture declares that,

> *When two full years had passed, **Pharaoh had a dream**: He was standing by the Nile, when out of the river there came up seven cows, sleek and fat, and they grazed among the reeds... And the cows that were ugly and gaunt ate up the seven sleek, fat cows. **Then Pharaoh woke up.***
>
> ***He fell asleep again and had a second dream**: Seven ears of corn, healthy and good, were growing on a single stalk... The thin ears of corn swallowed up the seven healthy, full ears. Then Pharaoh woke up; it had been a dream.*
> **Genesis 41:1-7, emphasis mine.**

But there are also cases where dreams are repeated within a week, a month, a year or during lengthy period of one's existence. Repeated dreams ought to be noted and given special attention. In Joseph's interpretation of Pharaoh's repeated dream, he stated that the reason for Pharaoh's repeated dream was because *"the matter [that is, what Pharaoh dreamed about] has been firmly decided by God, and God will do it soon"* (Genesis 41:32).

This means a repeated dream conveys the idea that whatever the dream means has been firmly determined to happen. Such a dream is sure to happen (whether positive or negative) if nothing is done to avert its occurrence. It also means that whatever such dream means and speaks of is certain to happen in the nearest future. Thus, repetition of dream implies certainty of its occurrence in the nearest future. It doesn't mean it cannot be averted. Its occurrence depends on the attitude of the dreamer and those concerned, and their knowledge and ability to tackle such dream especially when such dream is negative. Joseph, by divine wisdom, was able to stop the devastating effects of the seven years famine Pharaoh dreamed of. The famine came, but the people survived. Nobody died from starvation because there was enough food for all Egyptians including foreigners. The famine meant to devastate the nation of Egypt eventually enriched Pharaoh and his kingdom. The intended misfortune became a great fortune.

1

Biblical Teachings on Dreams 1

There is no book in the entire world that shed greater light on the subject of dream like the Bible. The Scripture records men who had dreams, their dreams and corresponding interpretations. It also records certain teachings that serve as guidelines and directives on this subject of dream. In this chapter, I dealt with dream as a state, and analyzed the dreams of people whose dreams were recorded in the Scripture.

Dream is a State

As a dream when one wakes, so when you arise,
O Lord, you will despise them as fantasies.
Psalm 73:20, emphasis mine.

A dream is a state. In that state the human body is asleep. Sleep never implies inactivity and unconsciousness. This is because when a person sleeps, one sometimes rolls, mumbles and as expected, except dead, breathes continuously. Some fellows snore while asleep. The sleeping person might be unconscious of on going activities within the physical environment and world. But the sleeper's non-involvement and participation in physical activities cannot be correctly adjudged as unconsciousness. While asleep, his organs still fulfill some vital functions of an active, living person. For instance, the sleeper still breathes, perspires, rolls (that is, moves some parts of his or her physical body), feels (either comfortable or uncomfortable and reacts to mosquitoes' bites depending on the environment), and even hears (when screamed at at close range).

In this sleeping condition a person dreams. In dream, the sleeper experiences all the various activities and experiences an active, living person experiences in a physical, natural world. In the dream, the sleeper, now a dreamer is exposed to either familiar or unfamiliar environment. In this environment, the dreamer encounters familiar and strange persons and creatures, sometimes creatures he or she has never seen on earth.

The dreamer hears words and sometimes engages in discussions, interactions, and experiences relationship and even hostility. Sometimes these come as images, pictures and films that the dreamer looks at or participates in or in some cases a combination of both. In this realm, the dreamer sometimes dresses gorgeously or tattered. Sometimes, the dreamer appears nude or half naked.

These occurrences sometimes come in long or short scenes. Some scenes continue to the end, while others are brief and different. In some cases, these scenes may be multiple and clear or multiple and bizarre. The duration of each scene is either long or brief.

The dreamer is in no position to determine the duration of anything in a dream. The only thing a dreamer has influence over is his or her imaged person, and subjectively, the activities the dreamer gets involved in a dream. This, to a large extent, is determined by the dreamer's spiritual, physical and psychological state, and his or her experiences in the physical, natural world.

The range of activities and experiences that occur in a dream are beyond any human's imagination. In dream, a dreamer might experience past events involving ancient persons, sometimes never seen physically. A dreamer might also encounter present events and persons, and also future persons and events that a dreamer has no clue of. In this realm, a person's spirit especially a Christian is more alert, discerning and knowledgeable sometimes than in the physical realm.

This state is never permanent. It obviously comes to an end with time. Then the dreamer eventually awakes. On awakening, the dreamer's alertness and consciousness in the dream state is tasked. The dreamer either remembers or sometimes completely forgets the dream. In some cases, the dreamer recalls only bits and pieces of such a dream(s). And may be in the process of time, the dreamer eventually remembers a large fragment of that dream or the complete dream. This may probably account for king Nebuchadnezzar's enigmatic demand on his magicians, enchanters, sorcerers and astrologers (Daniel 2:1-11). The Scripture asserts that when Nebuchadnezzar had gathered his magicians, enchanters, sorcerers and astrologers together, he declared,

> *This is what I have firmly decided: If you do not tell me what my dream was and interpret it, I will have you cut into pieces and your houses turned into piles of rubble. But if you tell me the dream and explain it, you will receive from me gifts and rewards and great honour. So tell me the dream and interpret it for me.*
> **Daniel 2:5-6.**

Once awakened, one begins to ponder on the reality, originality, tangibility and actuality of the event(s) dreamt of. It is this puzzle that has driven several people to different perspectives, opinions and conclusions on the subject called dream. Nevertheless, I must assert that dream is a world of its own where persons, things and events are dressed in both usual and unusual ways. The appearance of persons, things, events, and the fluidity and rapidity of dream's happenings, most times, beat people's imagination and leave them aghast. Consequently, some people fail to realize that dream is indeed another world within a person's pneuma-psycho-physiological world[¶]. Dream is a world of mysteries. Unravel it.

People Who had Dreams in the Scripture.

There are at least fourteen people who had dreams in the Scripture. They included kings and servants, men and women, Gentiles and Jews, and believers and non-believers in the God of the Bible. They are listed below in the order of the biblical books. But I'll like to encourage you as my reader at this junction to please take up your Bible and read all the underlisted references. This will enable you have a good grasp of these dreams as I'll from henceforth assume that you have a good understanding of the several dreams recorded in the Bible. Thus I'll only cite such references without further explication.

1. Abimelech, a Gentile king (Genesis 20:3-7,8,17,18).
2. Jacob, one of the Jewish patriarchs (Genesis 28:12-15; 31:10-13).
3. Laban, Jacob's uncle (Genesis 31:24).

[¶] Pneuma-psycho-physiological world refers to a person's spiritual, psychological and physiological world. This describes the spiritual, mental and bodily process occurring in a person.

4. Joseph, a Jew who became a prime minister in Egypt (Genesis 37:5-7, 9).
5. Pharaoh's cupbearer (butler), a Gentile (Genesis 40:5,9-13).
6. Pharaoh's chief baker, a Gentile (Genesis 40:5,16-22).
7. Pharaoh, the Egyptian monarch (Genesis 41:1-7,17-27,29-40).
8. A Midianite soldier (Judges 7:13-15).
9. Solomon, Israel's wisest and wealthiest king (1 Kings 3:5-15).
10. Nebuchadnezzar, one of the ancient world's most powerful Gentile kings (Daniel 2:1-3,31-47; 4:5,9-37).
11. Daniel, an Israelite exile who became a prophet and prominent statesman in three Gentile kingdoms (Daniel 7:1-28).
12. Joseph, the foster father of our Lord Jesus Christ (Matthew 1:18- 24; 2:13,14,19-23).
13. The wise men from the east (Matthew 2:12).
14. Pilate's wife, a Gentile woman (Matthew 27:19).

A brief analysis of these individuals' dreams shows the wide range of life activities covered in their dreams. This analysis reveals that dreams, when properly understood, can be used by God to address various aspects and issues of our lives. It also shows that irrespective of our race, nationality, sex and social status in life, God can sometimes speak to us through our dreams depending on our understanding of dream.

There are several things God accomplished through the dreams mentioned above in the lives of individuals, families, and nations and the world at large. And I believe these things can be repeated in our lives, and much more, if only we can allow God to use this same medium of dream to minister to us.

Divine Warning and Directive

In the Bible, God gave divine warnings and directives to people through dreams. Among the individuals whose dreams were recorded in Scripture, four received divine warnings and directives. These are Abimelech, Laban, the wise men from the east, and Joseph, the foster father of our Lord Jesus Christ.

Abimelech, after unknowingly taking Sarah, Abraham's wife to be one of his wives, was warned by God in a dream not to touch her but to restore her to Abraham her rightful husband. And then he was also instructed to ask Abraham to pray for him and his entire household to deliver them from death, and all the women in his household from barrenness. According to Genesis 20:7, God instructed Abimelech to *"return the man's wife, for he is a prophet, and he will pray for you and you will live. But if you do not return her, you may be sure that you and all yours will die."* When Abimelech obeyed and carried out God's instruction, *"Then Abraham prayed to God, and God healed Abimelech, his wife and his slave girls so they could have children again, for the LORD had closed up every womb in Abimelech's household because of Abraham's wife Sarah"* (Genesis 20:17-18). Laban also received warning restraining him from whatever he intended to do against Jacob. The Scripture declares, *"Then God came to Laban the Aramean in a dream at night and said to him, 'Be careful not to say anything to Jacob, either good or bad'"* (Genesis 31:24).

In the New Testament, Joseph was instructed and warned twice by an angel of the Lord in dreams. Joseph's reception of Mary as his wife was based on the instruction he got from dream (Mathew 1:20-21,24). Joseph was also warned on two occasions: first, on Herod's attempt to assassinate the child Jesus, and second, as to where to live and raise up Jesus in line with biblical prophecy (Matthew 2:13,19-23). The wise men from the east were also warned in a dream not to return to Herod (Matthew 2:12).

Can you imagine what would have been the fatal results of each of these averted disasters, beginning from Abimelech to Joseph? Just imagine being married to one of the ladies from Abimelech's household if they were not prayed for or the idea of Joseph refusing to accept Mary as his wife and exposing her to public shame. And then imagine how many lives and marriages could and can be saved, and how many shame and wrong acts can be averted if Christians can exploit this God-given medium of dream?

Divine Encounter

Divine encounter most times results in the transformation of an individual's life and worldview. Two individuals through dream experienced divine encounter in the Scripture. They were Jacob and Solomon. Jacob, in a dream, had a personal revelation of God and had the covenant promise transformed to him (Genesis 28:12-15). In another dream, he was instructed to return to the land of promise (Genesis 31:10-13). These dreams strengthened the patriarch's faith and walk with God.

Solomon, through a dream, was endowed with divine wisdom and wealth (1 Kings 3:5-14). When he awoke from this dream, his life and reign never remained the same. He eventually emerged as the wisest and wealthiest man and king time had ever witnessed. Only eternity can reveal how many lives had been transformed through dreams. Our God can still transform personal lives and worldviews and strengthen our faith and walk with Him today through dreams. He is only waiting for His children to avail themselves of this medium and exploit it.

Jacob and Solomon believed their dreams, walked in them and enjoyed the dividends. What about you? Do you believe your dreams? Can you afford to walk in it?

Divine Revelation of Destiny

Destiny is a blueprint of God's plan and purpose for an individual's life. Destiny is one of the major talks of our present generation. In Scripture, Joseph and Nebuchadnezzar both had their destiny revealed in dreams. Joseph's dreams like capsules captured in summary what he became in the future (Genesis 37:5-7,9). Through dreams, Joseph realized he was destined to be a leader.

In one dream, Nebuchadnezzar caught a glimpse of his greatness, his demotion, and future restoration to greatness (Daniel 4:5,10-17,20-26). The Bible records the exact fulfillment of Nebuchadnezzar's dream.

A revelation of one's destiny will instill hope, courage and great motivation in a person's life's pursuit especially when such a destiny is worthy. Such a dream can dispel darkness and frustration. What a joy to know what you are and will become before it eventually comes true! Dream can afford you this joy.

Divine Revelation of Fate

Fate here implies an inevitable outcome. My choice of this word stems from the final outcome of the butler's and baker's lives. In one night, Pharaoh's cupbearer (butler) and baker each had a dream. Their dreams detailed what fate had ahead of them in just three days (Genesis 40:5,9-13,16-22). The butler's face brightened when Joseph's interpretation of his dream pointed to a bright future. Just imagine what enthusiasm filled him for the three days before his restoration. Dream has the power to determine your emotional state in life.

The book of Judges records a Midianite's soldier's dream and his friend's interpretation (Judges 7:13-15). His friend's interpretation of his own dream spells self-defeat and doom for their own nation, Midian. The Midianites were eventually defeated by Gideon and his three hundred men. I am sure the Midianite soldier and his friend went into the battle dispirited and self-defeated. Dream can predict the outcome of a person's future venture or adventure.

Divine Revelation of World Events

The God of the Bible is the God of the whole world and He reveals world events. Through dreams, God revealed world events to three individuals recorded in the Scripture. These individuals were Pharaoh, Nebuchadnezzar and Daniel.

In the era of the last Jewish patriarch, Jacob, God saved the then world from a global food crisis (famine) through dreams to Pharaoh, interpreted by Joseph (Genesis 41:1-7,17-27,29-31). A global food crisis was averted by a dream given and correctly interpreted.

Both Nebuchadnezzar and Daniel received a revelation of the kingdoms of this world designed to operate for generations. The span of these kingdoms ranged from the Babylonian kingdom to the Roman empire and to the establishment and dominion of Christ's kingdom (Daniel 2:1-3,31-45). Daniel's dream was more detailed (Daniel 7:1-14,17-27). These dreams have formed a major portion of end-time events. These were men who through dreams, saw not just tomorrow, but the future and the end.

Their dreams distinguished them. Your dreams can also distinguish you. You can see beyond the present and see the future. There is a God in heaven who reveals mysteries (Daniel 2:28), and He can through dreams reveal your tomorrow, your future.

A Nightmare

Only Pilate's wife's dream could be termed a nightmare (Matthew 27:19). Her own description of her night experience warrants the name "nightmare". Whatever the name, one truth stands out, she got the message, *"Have nothing to do with that righteous Man"* (NASB). The dream left her with a message. Dream is designed to convey message to people. Your dream speaks, find out the message.

2

Biblical Teachings on Dreams II

This chapter continues our study on biblical teachings on dreams. Here I examined the sources of dreams, types of dreams, what dreams can do to a person, and the purposes of dreams as exposed in the Scripture.

Sources of Dreams

From the records of Scripture, dreams can be traced to five sources. These sources cover the divine aspect of life (deity, that is, God), the world of spirits, and man's physical and psychological components. These sources are enumerated below.

1. *God.* This is the first and foremost source of dreams. As the Creator of mankind, God is also the Creator and Designer of dream. He specifically designed dream as a medium for speaking to His people, especially His servants. In reprimanding Aaron and Miriam, God openly declares, *"listen to my words: 'When a prophet of the LORD is among you, I reveal myself to him in visions, I speak to him in dreams'"* (Numbers 12:6). Daniel, in interpreting Nebuchadnezzar's dream, declares, *"The great God has shown the king what will take place in the future. The dream is true and the interpretation is trustworthy"* (Daniel 2:45). God speaks through dreams. He reveals through dreams. What He speaks through dreams we ought to hear. And whatever He reveals through dreams, we ought to find out. But unfortunately, men do not perceive. *"For God does speak–now one way, now another–though man*

may not perceive it. In a dream, in a vision of the night, when deep sleep falls on men as they slumber in their beds, he may speak in their ears ..." (Job 33:14-16). God can speak to you through dreams. So be open.

2. *Much Work (Busyness).* This points to the psychological make-up of a person. Ecclesiastes identifies much work (busyness) as another source of dreams. *"For a dream cometh through the multitude of business"* (Ecclesiastes 5:3a KJV). Another version reads, *"For dreams result from much work"* (Ecclesiastes 5:3a HCSB). The *New Living Translation* reads, *"Just as being too busy gives you nightmares"* (Ecclesiastes 5:3a). The *New International Version* equated this with "many cares" – "anxiety". Whatever it is, this is projection of a person's state of mind. This is the kind of dream that science is well acquainted with. Most Dictionaries' definitions of dream spring from this source of dreams. Sleeping with unfinished work loads and sometimes pressing work loads could result into dreams. Prioritize your programmes.

3. *Hunger and Thirst.* This is another outshoot of our human composition. Some persons do dream when they sleep either hungry or thirsty, and sometimes, when they are overfed. The Scripture declares that *"as when a hungry man dreams that is he is eating, but he awakens and his hunger remains, as when a thirsty man dreams that he is drinking, but he awakens faint, with his thirst unquenched"* (Isaiah 29:8). The content of the dream reveals the person's physical and psychological condition. Some people, including Christians, who suffer from the experience of eating in dreams have this problem of either sleeping hungry with desire for food or eating late or overfeeding. This exposes them to this kind of dreams. There are

exceptional cases that should be discerned. Notwithstanding, plan your life. There is time for everything under the sun including eating. Don't starve yourself if you are not fasting.

4. *Thoughts.* A person's thought prepares and exposes him or her to dream. Whatever a person meditates on prior sleeping will to a large extent determine what he or she dreams. Concerning Nebuchadnezzar's dream, Daniel explained, *"As you were lying there, O king, your mind turned to things to come, and the revealer of mysteries showed you what is going to happen ... but so that you, O king, may know the interpretation and that you may understand what went through your mind..."* (Daniel 2:29,30). Nebuchadnezzar's thoughts focused on the future of his kingdom, and God revealed to him future kingdoms. Your thoughts can open you to divine revelation through dreams. Meditate on heavenly things and you will dream of heaven, its owner and dwellers. Meditate on biblical issues and events and you will dream of them. Good dreams, most times, spring from good thoughts. Your dreams might be revealing your thought-life.

5. *The Devil and His Cohorts.* To most Africans, the roles of the devil and his cohort of evil spirits and wicked human agents in dreams are no news. It is commonly believed in Africa that most nightmares have their roots in satanic manipulations. The Scripture alludes to this possibility when it announces the emergence of a dreamer whose intention is to deceive God's people. Deuteronomy 13:1-5 assert,

> *If a prophet, or one who foretells by dreams, appears among you and announces to you a miraculous sign or wonder, and if the sign or*

> *wonder of which he has spoken takes place, and he says, "Let us follow other gods" (gods you have not known) "and let us worship them," you must not listen to the words of that prophet or dreamer... That prophet or dreamer must be put to death....*

The devil and his cohorts can and do manipulate people through dreams. Be discerning in your dreams and their interpretations. Some have been led astray by fake dreams.

Types of Dreams

Dreams are classified based on our ability to discern their source(s), their interpretations, and the possibility of their happening. Dreams could be classified into three types. These are positive, negative and empty dreams.

Positive Dreams

A dream can be termed positive when it springs either from God or positive thoughts or both; when its interpretation is good, that is, positive and it is sure to come true. In Genesis, Pharaoh's cupbearer (butler) had a dream that Joseph interpreted as promising and heart warming (Genesis 40:9-13). The dream and its interpretation points to a bright tomorrow and gives the butler a hope of restoration to Pharaoh's service. The Scripture says when the chief baker saw that *"the interpretation was positive"* (Genesis 40:16 HCSB) that is, good and favourable, he was motivated to share his dream.

Positive dreams are good dreams. They are favourable ones. They give hope and cast a bright future. They are motivational to the dreamer and others especially non-rivals. They strengthen and encourage a person. They give you a reason to live. Jacob, Joseph, Pharaoh's butler, Solomon and Daniel all had positive dreams. God gave them. You too can have positive dreams. I pray God open your eyes and connect you to positive dreams.

Positive dream can become a person's life vision and aspiration. Joseph's dream was his life goal and aspiration. Positive dream can change a person's life and worldview. It changed Jacob's life and worldview (Genesis 28:16-22). Positive dreams can save a person, a family and a nation. Abimelech's dream saved him and his entire household. Pharaoh's dream saved him, his kingdom, and the then world from a global food crisis.

Positive dream can make you great. Joseph's dream made him a leader, prime minister in Egypt. Solomon's dream made him the wisest and wealthiest man and king the earth has ever known. Daniel's dreams made him an end-time prophet and eschatologist. Joseph's dream saved his marriage and our Saviour's life.

Negative Dreams

These are the opposite of positive dreams. They neither spring from God nor good thoughts. They come from the devil and his cohorts, and from evil thoughts, and also have the propensity to come true when left unattended to. Their interpretation without being told is negative, bad, evil and disheartening. The chief baker's dream and its interpretation were negative. Genesis 40:16-19 assert,

When the chief baker saw that the interpretation was positive, he said to Joseph, "I also had a

> *dream. Three baskets of white bread were on my head. In the top basket were all sorts of baked goods for Pharaoh, but the birds were eating them out of the basket on my head."*
>
> *"This is the interpretation," Joseph replied, "The three baskets are three days. In just three days Pharaoh will lift up your head – from off you – and hang you on a tree. Then the birds will eat the flesh from your body.* **[HCSB].**

The fulfillment of his dream and its interpretation cost him his office and his life. Genesis 40:20,22 assert that on the third day which was Pharaoh's birthday, he lifted up the heads of the chief cupbearer and the chief baker in the presence of all his officials, "but hanged the chief baker, just as Joseph had said to them in his interpretation."

Negative dreams are bad dreams. They are unfavourable. They fill a person with fear and despair. They are terrifying and perplexing. They fill the dreamer and others with fear and hopelessness. They paralyze a person and render him or her speechless and dumbfounded. They cast a dark spell on a person's future and career. They are some of the devil's strongest means of accomplishing his evil triple agenda. John 10:10 asserts. *"The thief [devil] comes only to steal and kill and destroy."*

Negative dreams can demoralize a person's spirit and dampen a person's hope and courage. Negative dreams speak and spread self-defeat and discouragement. It dispirited the Midianite soldier and his colleague and eventually brought defeat and destruction. Negative dreams can disturb, dispossess and destroy. It disturbed Pharaoh's chief baker, dispossessed him of his office and then killed him. Negative dreams can restrain and limit. It restrained and limited Laban's achievement on a seven day pursuit. Laban and his relatives returned empty-handed. Negative dreams can demote and depose. It banished Nebuchadnezzar from his kingship and kingdom for seven years.

Negative dreams can torment and torture. Pilate's wife suffered torture in and from a negative dream. Don't leave negative dreams unattended to. Deal with them. Don't be ignorant of the devil's devices, negative dreams are one of his devices (2 Corinthians 2:11 KJV).

Empty Dreams

For the idols speak falsehood, and the diviners see illusions; ***they relate empty dreams and offer empty comfort.*** *Therefore the people wander like sheep; they suffer affliction because there is no shepherd.*
Zechariah 10:2 HCSB, emphasis mine.

Empty dreams, as the name implies, are dreams that can't and will never deliver any inspired hope. They may promise greatness, success, and a better tomorrow but these promises never come to pass. Dreams inspired by much work, busyness, anxiety, and either hunger and thirst or late eating or overfeeding are empty dreams. They may stir up hope or fear, but never deliver. They are like false prophecy. They lack the power of fulfillment. They are illusions. These are like mirages, and springs without water and mists driven by a storm. They are clouds without water. Empty dreams, most times, are bizarre in nature. And even when clear in vision, they are meaningless and without any interpretation. For some people, most of their dreams fall in this class. Their dreams are just empty. They have no substance, no meaning and no interpretation. They only just sometimes deprive the dreamer a good night rest. May God grant any reader who is exposed to this experience deliverance today in Jesus' name. Amen. Enjoy sound sleep from now on in Jesus' name. Amen.

What Dreams can do to a Person

Dreams can inspire certain emotional reactions in a dreamer and sometimes in its listeners (hearers) depending on the listener's relation to such dreams. The emotional reactions stir in a dreamer to a large extent is determined by the nature and type of dream he or she had. Below are some of the emotional reactions a dream can stir in a person.

First, *a dream can trouble a person.* Pharaoh's dream troubled him when he awoke in the morning (Genesis 41:8). This was probably due to the nature of his dream. Nebuchadnezzar had a dream that troubled him that he could not sleep (Daniel 2:1). His dream drove sleep from him. A person's dream can deprive him or her sleep and trouble him or her until interpretation and meaning is found.

Second, *a dream can frighten and terrify.* When Abimelech shared his dream with his servants, they were terrified (Genesis 20:8 HCSB). When Jacob, through dream, discovered that where he slept was heaven's gate, he was afraid (Genesis 28:17 HCSB). Nebuchadnezzar's own dream frightened him (Daniel 4:5 HCSB). Daniel's dream and the angel's interpretation of the dream's happenings terrified his thoughts and turned his face pale when he got up (Daniel 7:28 HCSB).

Third, *a dream can make a person sad and worry.* The dreams of Pharaoh's cupbearer (butler) and baker changed their mood and countenance when they woke up. They were dejected and looked sad when Joseph came into the ward (Genesis 40:6,7). An uninterpreted dream has the power to steal a person's joy and brightness. Contrariwise, *a good dream and its interpretation can stir up joy and rejoicing in a person.*

Fourth, *a dream can earn a person (most times the dreamer) hatred.* Joseph's brothers hated him because of his dreams (Genesis 37:8). Sometimes, the hatred may be the dreamer's depending on what is dreamed. When the devil operates by impersonation in a dream, an undiscerning dreamer can develop hatred for the individual impersonated. Don't hate a person because of any dream. Hatred is a murderous disposition (1 John 3:14,15). Guard against it in your heart. Love builds up. Hatred destroys.

Fifth, *a dream can lead to mockery.* Joseph's brothers mocked him because of his dreams. Genesis 37:19 records their mockery when it notes their comments to each other: "Here comes that dreamer!" People can nickname you because of your dreams. Be careful who you share your dreams with. Most people will not appreciate your dreams of greatness, success and elevation until they materialize.

Sixth, *a dream can propel a plan and preparation for the future.* This is one of God's major aims in dreams. From Pharaoh's own dream, Joseph drew a 14 year plan that saved his world from famine (Genesis 41:28-37). Joseph's dream prompted an immediate exodus to Egypt to save the baby Jesus (Matthew 2:13-14). Positive dreams call for planning and preparation for the future.

Purposes of Dreams

There are several reasons God gives dreams to His people. These reasons are the purposes of dreams. Every positive dream has defined purpose(s). Whatever medium of communication God designed for His people is used to communicate messages, divine and profitable ones. Dreams speak and what they speak are messages. A profitable message is a message understood (1 Corinthians 14:6-11). Therefore, in dream, we should strive to know and understand the message it is intended to communicate.

Positive dreams communicate positive and profitable messages. But negative dreams communicate negative and unprofitable messages. We must understand that the devil and his cohorts will use the medium of dreams to communicate their evil messages. God in His infinite wisdom allows this because when we lean on the Spirit's understanding and through His help discern the message behind a dream, we are able to discern the enemy's scheme(s). Negative dreams, when allowed by God, are intended to expose the devil and his cohorts' evil plans and schemes.

In the overall, God allows dreams whether positive or negative for the following reasons.

1. *To warn a person.* Job 33:16 asserts, *"he may speak in their ears and terrify them with warnings."* This warning may be of an impending disaster like that of Abimelech when he took Sarah, Abraham's wife (Genesis 20:3). This warning saved Abimelech from the sin of adultery. This act, according to God's message in the dream, is tantamount to death and the resultant barrenness of every female in his household (Genesis 20:18). These disasters were averted when Abimelech understood God's message in the dream,

and acted as instructed by God in his dream. Also, Laban's intended act against Jacob was also averted by the warning he received in his dream (Genesis 31:24). In a dream a person can be warned by God to desist from an intended act. Please, when warned, heed warnings from dreams.

2. *To change a person's course of action.* Job 33:17a asserts, *"to turn man from wrongdoing,"* This is as a result of the message received from the dream. Abimelech originally took Sarah to be one of his wives without knowing she was Abraham's wife. And as one of his wives, his intention was to lie with her. But this changed when he discovered through dream that she was Abraham's wife. He returned Sarah to Abraham (Genesis 20:7,14). His course of action changed and he saved his life and the lives of his entire household. One dream can change a person's course of action and save many.

I remember when I was employed as a pastor in a church and placed on three months' probation. After three months, the probation continued. I decided I was going to confront my senior pastor, insisting that I be posted to the promised post of duty. I decided this confrontation will be the next day, Sunday after service. But that night, I had a dream and its message rebuked and restrained my desired course of action. Immediately, I changed my course of action. A month later I was asked to take the Bible study which eventually led to my appointment as the assistant pastor while another was sent to that station. That dream stopped my action that was against God's plan for me. One dream can change a lot of things and situations in a person's life when its message is clearly and properly understood.

3. *To suppress a person's pride.* Job 33:17b asserts, *"and keep him from pride."* Pride is competitive and destructive in nature. God resists pride (1 Peter 5:5-6). But unfortunately, most, if not all men, are prone to pride. There are several things that instill pride in a person. In a dream, God exposed Nebuchadnezzar's pride due to his greatness and through its interpretation revealed to him what it will cost him (Daniel 4:23-26). But unfortunately, Nebuchadnezzar refused to listen to the voice of wisdom and barely after a year of his dream, he fell prey to pride. He was banished to a seven year course at "Forest Theological Seminary" to be tutored by animals and vegetations and to learn that the Most High rules in the affairs of men (Daniel 4:29-33).

Nebuchadnezzar's dream was intended to suppress pride in him. Unfortunately, he couldn't resist the force of pride and humble himself. His greatness swollen his head and stiffened his elbows until God humiliated and humbled him. He eventually graduated with a PhD in Divine Sovereignty (Daniel 4:34-37). Pride robbed him of his throne, and stripped him of his greatness for seven years. Just imagine what Nebuchadnezzar would have accomplished in those seven years. Only eternity can tell. Rid yourself of pride before it ruins you.

4. *To spare a person's life.* Job 33:18 declares, *"to preserve his soul from the pit, his life from perishing by the sword."* Life is a precious gift from God and He takes no pleasure in its destruction (Ezekiel 33:11). God wills to spare people's lives from death. Dream is one medium He uses to communicate and do this. Through dreams God intends to save people's lives from physical, spiritual and eternal death. When a person clearly comprehends God's message in a dream and heeds its warnings (if there are any), such a life is spared from "the pit" (a metonymy for spiritual and

eternal death) and "the sword" (another metonymy for physical death) (Job 33:18).

Through a dream, Abimelech and his entire household were preserved from death (Genesis 20:7,17-18). Through dreams, Pharaoh, his kingdom (Egypt) and the then world were preserved from death by famine (Genesis 41:30,36; 45:5-7). Through a dream, God spared baby Jesus from Herod's brutal massacre (Matthew 2:13-14). A dream can be used by God as a means to save lives. He still does today.

5. To give a person a glimpse of his or her destiny. Destinies are sometimes encapsulated in positive dreams. Your destiny is God's blueprint for your life. God gives positive dreams. These positive dreams are sometimes like glimpses of our tomorrow and the future of our world. These kinds of dreams cast images, pictures of a bright, positive future for a person. When a dream casts an image of a bright, positive future, God intends it to become a vision, goal and an aspiration for the future. Joseph caught this message and aspired for a brighter tomorrow. He dreamed he was a leader and that people paid homage to him (Genesis 37:5-10). This dream distinguished him as a leader wherever he found himself (Genesis 39:1-6,21-23).

Finally, his dream of a prominent and powerful leader came true when Pharaoh made him next to himself (Genesis 41:39-45). You can make you positive dreams a vision for the future. Turn your positive dreams into life vision and pursuits. Don't idolize your positive dreams like Nebuchadnezzar (Daniel 2:31-33,37-43 cf 3:1-6) or you might end up worshipping them. Turn your positive dreams into life's aspiration. Then you will profit from your dreams (Genesis 50:15-21)

6. To enable a person plan and prepare for the future. Our God knows the future and plans for it. In Jeremiah 29:11, the Lord declares, *"For I know the plans I have for you, plans to prosper you and not to harm you, plans to give you hope and a future."* He gives positive dreams like glimpses of our tomorrow and the future of our world. These glimpses in dreams are meant to stir up within a person a plan and preparation for the future. Joseph drew a 14 year plan from Pharaoh's own dreams that saved his world from famine (Genesis 41:28-37).

Most positive dreams have action plans. Figure out the plan and run with it. It can distinguish you. Positive dreams, most times, are God's blueprints for the future. Grasp the revelation. Unravel the mystery. Then draw a plan for your future. Preparation begins immediately you discover the plan. In the New Testament, Joseph's dream prompted an immediate exodus to Egypt to save the baby Jesus (Matthew 2:13-14). Positive dreams call for planning and preparations for the future. Sometimes prompt actions like Joseph's are needed to actualize your dream.

3

How to tackle Dreams

It is one thing to dream, it is another to know how to handle and tackle your dreams. Apart from empty dreams, positive and negative dreams need to be tackled appropriately because they have the potential to come true. Thus, these dreams should not be swept aside like empty dreams.

Positive and negative dreams convey messages that can come true either in the near or distant future. These messages also affect the dreamer, his family and his world at large. Joseph's dream of being a leader came true. Pharaoh's dreams of seven year abundance and another seven year famine both came true. The dreams of Pharaoh's cupbearer (butler) and chief baker came true. Solomon's dream came true when he eventually emerged the wisest and wealthiest monarch the earth has ever witnessed. The list continues.

When we have awakened from our dreams and can recall them whether they are positive or negative by nature and interpretation, we must ensure we do any of the following that is appropriate depending on the type of dream and its interpretation.

1. *Be careful who you share your dream(s) with.* Your dreams are yours and the choice of sharing is yours. The kind of dream a person has should determine with whom you share it. Remember, your dream especially of elevation, success and greatness may not excite everyone. Joseph's brothers hated him for his dream to the extent they couldn't speak a kind word to him (Genesis 37:4). Joseph's dreams made his brothers to

mock and conspire against him (Genesis 37:19-20). The Scripture records, that when they saw Joseph coming, they said to each other, *"Here comes that dreamer! Come now, let's kill him and throw him into one of these cisterns and say that a ferocious animal devoured him. Then we will see what comes of his dreams"*(Genesis 37:19-20). Let wisdom guard and guide in your choice of who to share your dream(s) with.

2. *Keep your dreams, especially positive ones, in mind.* Joseph's destiny unfolded amidst two dreams, his personal dreams and Pharaoh's. Joseph dreamt he was a leader people paid homage to. This dream triggered his brother's jealousy, hatred and conspiracy. When he shared his dream, the Scripture records that, while his brothers became jealous of him, his father Jacob *"kept the matter [Joseph's dream] in mind"* (Genesis 37:11). I am very sure Joseph also kept his dreams in mind. Remember, Joseph's dream became his life's vision and pursuit. Resultantly, he always emerged a leader whenever he found himself. The prison couldn't stop him. A focused vision cannot be killed, stopped or imprisoned. Even in prison Joseph was a leader (Genesis 39:20-23).

His dreamed vision of a prominent and powerful leader found fulfillment in his interpretation of Pharaoh's dreams (Genesis 41:39-45). When Joseph emerged next to Pharaoh, I am certain he saw a part fulfillment of his dream. Now a national leader with global influence, notwithstanding he is yet to see his brothers pay homage to him. In Genesis 42:5-8, when his brothers arrived in his presence and bowed with their faces to the ground before him, the Scripture says, *"then he remembered his dreams about them"* (Genesis 42:9). He finally saw the complete fulfillment of his dreams, a prominent and powerful leader to who people paid homage including his brothers. Your dream of greatness will come true. Nothing can stop it. It may look delayed but time will work to manifest and fulfill it. Keep your positive dreams in mind. Let them trigger your daily pursuit until you see the complete manifestation and fulfillment. Good dreamers and visionaries keep their dreams and visions in mind.

3. *Interpret your dreams either by yourself or through an interpreter.* There are a lot of funny things happening in the Christian faith today in the name of interpretation of dreams. It is important to note that there are no biblically approved formulae for interpreting dreams. Every dream recorded and interpreted within Scripture is first and foremost by divine light shed in the interpreters' hearts. Both Joseph and Daniel, individuals distinguished by their ability to understand and interpret dreams, remarked that interpretation of dreams comes from God. In Genesis 41:16, when Pharaoh declared that he learnt Joseph can interpret dreams, Joseph debunked and asserted, *"I cannot do it, but **God will give Pharaoh the answer he desires"*** (emphasis mine). In Daniel 2:27,28, Daniel affirmed the same before Nebuchadnezzar when he asserted, *"No wise man, enchanter, magician or diviner can explain to the king the mystery he has asked about, **but there is a God in heaven who reveals mysteries"*** (emphasis mine). Whatever formula of interpretation a person uses to interpret dreams is limited and would one day expire like those of Nebuchadnezzar's and Pharaoh's enchanters, magicians, sorcerers and astrologers (Genesis 41:8; Daniel 2:27). There are only two broad classifications of interpretation for whatever dream a person has. These are positive or negative interpretations. Every dream can only be interpreted

positively or negatively. This is based on the source(s) and nature of the dream that obviously determine its type. Every positive dream has a positive interpretation. While every negative dream results in negative interpretation (Genesis 40:16,18-19).

You can interpret your dreams (most of them) yourself. Every born again Christian has the spirit of interpretation, the Holy Spirit dwelling within him or her. When a Christian dreams, he or she is still within that dream realm or world for the first five minutes or more after he or she awakes. His or her spirit is alert in the spiritual realm, and open to the Spirit's interpretation of his or her dream. The Holy Spirit is only waiting for you to ask Him and He will grant you the interpretation of your dream.

The key to interpreting your dream is calmness and spiritual alertness to the Holy Spirit the moment (especially the first five minutes or more) you awake from your dream. Unfortunately, some Christians don't even know how to hear from the Holy Spirit. The adversary, the devil and his cohorts also know this is the moment of interpretation. Thus, they have devised several things to militate against the Christian profiting from this moment.

Satanic Strategies to Hinder the Interpretation of Your Dream

There are several strategies the devil and his cohorts of evil spirits (demons) and wicked human agents have devised to ensure a dreamer, especially a Christian, does not receive the meaning and interpretation of his or her dream. Below are the most employed satanic strategies:

The devil's first strategy is to attempt to steal your dream or make you forget the dream before you awake from your sleep.

Second, if he is unsuccessful in this strategy in a Christian's life, he will ensure the Christian becomes dizzy and drowsy just after the dream or when trying to awake from his sleep. He will ensure the Christian feels tired, sleepy and procrastinate tackling the dream till a later hour. The key to overcoming this second strategy is to determine not to be slothful in business but fervent in spirit, serving the Lord (Romans 12:11 KJV). It is your God-given duty and service to attend to your dreams promptly. Don't allow the devil rob you of this vital moment to attend to your dreams. Remember, dreams convey messages and the Holy Spirit is willing and waiting on you to interpret your dreams. The Holy Spirit is the best interpreter of all types of dreams.

When this second strategy fails, the devil will use the third strategy of confusion, wandering and vagueness of mind. This is a situation where the Christian is awake quite alright, but his mind is confused as to what to do, wandering, just pacing, roaming the room and vague, not clear on what to do. You can't pray. You can't lay hands on anything or resolve to do a thing.

When this also fails, the devil attacks with fear. He frightens some Christians with their own dreams that they become paralyzed and inactive. They begin to meditate on what they must have done to deserve this negative dream or why the enemy wants to destroy them. I say, "You have done nothing" The fact that you are a Christian makes you the devil's prime target. Don't fear because *"God did not give us a spirit of timidity [fear], but a spirit of power, of love and self-discipline"* (2 Timothy 1:7). Rise up and fight the good fight of faith (1 Timothy 6:12).

When it is positive dream, the devil makes some Christians feel the dream is too good to be true. He tells them they have not done anything to earn or deserve such grand hope and destiny. He tells them the top of any walk of life is reserved for the spiritual or the best, and they are not. When they accept this satanic lie, they cancel the dream with their mouths and minds, and regard such a dream as impossible. In dream just like in life, a person's faith and choice counts (Matthew 9:29 KJV; 1 Thessalonians 5:21,22).

When all these fail to keep the Christian from attending to his or her dream, the devil preaches a seemingly spiritual, biblical sermon of fasting to the Christian. This he does by suggesting that the best way to tackle this dream is by coupling his prayers with fasting. So just go to sleep and today or tomorrow, depending on the time of the night, you can fast along to deal with the dream. Please, don't be labour yourself with any fast when you can deal with the dream here and now.

The devil has robbed Christians of this vital five minutes or more retention of that realm you dreamt about. Your spirit man is fully alert and ready to do spiritual warfare. Just maximize the opportunity. Believe your dreams. Remember all things are yours (1 Corinthians 3:21-23). Some Christians find it more convenient to believe evil, negative dreams than good, positive dreams. For instance, if some Christians dreamt they prayed for a lame man and in their dream, the lame man rose and walked. And in the same night they dreamed of being chased by cows. Some Christians will declare a fast believing some enemies are after their lives than to pray for the power to make lame people walk. Some will remark concerning a lame man walking when prayed for in dream that "it is just a dream". But for a cow chasing them, the remark is "they are planning to kill me". The Scripture says, *"Test everything. Hold on to the good [not the evil]"* (1 Thessalonians 5:21). Your response and reaction to dreams is determined by your convictions.

When unable to find the interpretation of your dream yourself, you can consult another Christian whom you know is mature and can be trusted. Share your dream with such a person. Whatever interpretation the individual gives must be judged in light of the Scripture. Isaiah 8:20 declares, *"To the law and to the testimony! If they do not speak according to this word, they have no light of dawn."* Here again, some Christians are also ignorant. When you can't judge the interpretation objectively by Scripture, try judging it subjectively by the inner witness and acceptance within your heart or inner person. I say acceptance because no interpreter has any final say on and over your dreams. You are the only person who has the final say. Your acceptance of whatever interpretation is given to your dream makes it binding (Matthew 16:19). So be careful how your dream is interpreted, and that includes your very self.

In the book of Judges 7:9-15, a Midianite soldier in camp, awaiting combat, dreamed of a loaf of bread tumbling into the Midianite camp destroying some tents among the camp. His friend's interpretation of this dream was horrible. He said, *"this [referring to the loaf of bread] can be nothing other than the sword of Gideon son of Joash, the Israelite. God has given the Midianites and the whole camp into his hands"* (Judges 7:14). Can you comprehend his interpretation? A loaf of bread equated to Gideon. Unbelievable! I just can't imagine it. This is the spirit of self-defeat in operation. The man and his friend accepted this interpretation and thousands died by the hands of Gideon and his three hundred men. What a horror and fate!

In addition to being careful how your dream is interpreted, you don't need to be silenced over negative interpretation of your dream. You, not the interpreter, have the final say. In Genesis 40:18-22, Joseph interpreted the dreams of Pharaoh's butler and chief baker. The butler's dream, Joseph interpreted positively and that of the chief baker, he interpreted negatively. Both men were silent over Joseph's interpretations of their dreams. This means they accepted his interpretation. They allowed Joseph to have the final say over their fate outside the prison. The Scripture records, *"but he [Pharaoh] hanged the chief baker, just as Joseph had said to them in his interpretation"* (Genesis 40:22).

Joseph's interpretation sealed their fate (destiny). Note, it was Joseph's interpretation, not God's interpretation that sealed their fate. Don't allow a fellow human to determine and seal your fate or destiny without doing anything. You have a major role to play in the interpretation of your dream.

You can accept or refuse anybody's interpretation of your dream that is at variance with God's revealed will for your life. The chief baker sold his right due to ignorance and died sheepishly. Sheepishly!? Yes, you heard me well. He died sheepishly. Just hold your breath for a moment and you will know why I said sheepishly.

A dream is not a prophecy. And so it should not be left unchallenged. Even a prophecy of doom can be averted when the believer knows his or her relationship with the Master. The prophecy that Hezekiah should put his house in order in preparation for his death was averted when he prayed (2 Kings 20:1-6), not to mention the interpretation of a dream. The chief baker died sheepishly because of ignorance. Again, the same Joseph when interpreting Pharaoh's dreams suggested plans on how to avert the negative dream and interpretation of a devastating famine (Genesis 41:29-31,33-36). There is always a way to averting negative dreams and interpretations. So let no man have the final say over your dreams and destiny. Whatever the interpretation, you alone have the final say over your dreams. The choice is yours and always will be.

4. Cancel negative dreams and interpretations. This is done either by rebuking or by applying it to your enemies. Joseph, in one of his dreams, dreamed that the sun, the moon and eleven stars were bowing down to him (Genesis 37:9). When he shared this dream, his father Jacob got the clue and interpretation, and he rebuked him. The Scripture notes, *"He told his father and brothers, but **his father rebuked him.** "*What kind of dream is this that you have had?" he said, "Are your mother and brothers and I going to bow down to the ground before you?" (Genesis 37:10 HCSB, emphasis mine). Joseph couldn't answer the father's question, and he couldn't refute his father's rebuke. His brothers all kept quiet and became jealous when they ought to have canceled such a dream with a rebuke like their father.

In the process of time, this dream came true. All his brothers bowed down before him several times (Genesis 42:6; 43:26,28; 44:14; 50:18), only the father, Jacob never did. But he blessed Joseph's master, Pharaoh and Joseph himself and his two sons, Ephraim and Manasseh (Genesis 47:7-10; 48:15-20). Don't ever keep quiet over negative dreams and interpretations. Silence, they say, is concession. Don't concede to any negative dream and interpretation. Speak out against them.

When I was growing as a boy, my father had several dreams about me, most of them negative. They concern being poisoned in school. I was a brilliant chap. My father, though a non Christian then, was gifted with dreams and their interpretations. There was hardly a person I could remember, apart from myself, that my father dreamed of and shared his dreams with, that such dreams never came to pass. I was not saved then. But unconsciously, I always say, "papa non be me. e non go happen", meaning "father, it is not me. It will never happen". And of a truth, none happened. You can stop negative dreams and their interpretations from being fulfilled in your life. Refute it. Rebuke it.

In addition to rebuking it, you can cancel negative dreams and interpretations by applying them to your enemies. When Nebuchadnezzar shared his dream of his future banishment from the kingdom with Daniel, Daniel instantly knew its meaning. He was greatly perplexed for a time, and his thoughts terrified him (Daniel 4:19a). When he recovered from his perplexity and fear, he applied the dream to Nebuchadnezzar's enemies. The Scripture observes that Beltshazzar, that is, Daniel answered, "My Lord, if only the dream applied to your enemies and its meaning to your adversaries!" (Daniel 4:19b).

Someone might retort that Nebuchadnezzar was still banished from the kingdom. Yes, that is true. But this is not the whole picture. Nebuchadnezzar was banished for two reasons. First, he failed to tackle this dream appropriately. He wasn't the one who applied this dream to his enemies. It was Daniel. There is no scriptural evidence that he imitated Daniel by repeating directly and firmly Daniel's application. Again, it should be observed that Daniel's application was firstly a wish and then conditional. Daniel's application began with the word "may" indicating his own wish, not Nebuchadnezzar's. I am not saying you should wishfully apply negative dreams and interpretations to your enemies. I say apply it to them. This means speaking authoritatively that it is my enemies that will die, be demoted and so on in Jesus' name. Remember that the power of life and death is in your tongue (Proverbs 18:21). Speak what you want in your life. Decree what you want come to pass in your life in line with God's revealed will for you in the Scripture.

Nebuchadnezzar ought to say at the end of Daniel's interpretation of his dream, "It is not me but my enemies that will be banished from the kingdom for seven years". Pray it out. Speak out what you want in your life. Don't allow your interpreter (a fellow human) to have the final say in your life. The choice is yours.

5. *Change your way of life.* This is the second reason Nebuchadnezzar was banished. At the end of Daniel's interpretation of his dream, Daniel advised Nebuchadnezzar to change his way of life. Daniel's advice to Nebuchadnezzar was, *"renounce your sins by doing what is right, and your wickedness by being kind to the oppressed. It may be that then your prosperity will continue"* (Daniel 4:27). This is godly counsel. If only Nebuchadnezzar had heeded this counsel, things would have changed. The story would have been different. But unfortunately, he didn't change his way of life.

When a dream speaks doom for a person over his lifestyle and the person is advised to change; the doom can only be averted when such a person changes his or her way of life. Cancellation by rebuking and application will not help. Change is the key to averting such dream. My dad was a chained smoker. One night he dreamed he died from poisoned cigarettes given to him by a woman. When he awoke from his dream, he recalled the dream and the exact image of the woman. When he got up the following morning, he immediately brought a pack of cigarettes and started smoking. In less than five minutes, the woman he dreamed of came with a pack of cigarettes for my dad. My dad received the pack quite okay. The woman lingered behind, insisting that my dad take a stick of cigarette from her pack to smoke. My dad refused that he cannot open her pack until he finished his own pack already opened.

After staying for almost two hours, she left. The moment she departed, my dad took his pack and the woman's pack of cigarettes and buried both including the stick of cigarettes he was smoking. That day marked the end of smoking for my dad. He quit smoking. He never smoked again until he became a Christian and eventually died. When a dream speaks of change, please change. You can avert the fulfillment of negative dreams and interpretations by changing your way of life.

Abimelech changed his course of action and saved his life and those of his entire household. Pharaoh appointed Joseph to effect the needed changes to save his kingdom and the then world from famine. In the New Testament, Joseph changed his residential location from Israel to Egypt to preserve the baby Jesus. You too can change. When your dream speaks of change, please change. Change is the only constant in the world.

6. *Believe positive dreams and act on them.* Most Christians are blessed with positive dreams, but some do not believe their dreams and act on them. When some Christians dreamed they traveled abroad and in the same night, dreamed they fell into a pit, some have the tendency toward believing the later dream. When such awake from sleep, they believe someone is out there to harm or destroy them. They will declare a fast over the dream wherein they fell in a pit. But for the

dream of traveling abroad, they can't believe it because they can't figure out how it will be made possible.

Doubt speaks in their hearts. They will soon realize that they have no relatives or friends abroad. They are from poor and wretched family background. They can't ever afford the transport fare abroad. Doubt confronts them with all the impossibilities. They have no connection whatsoever. They have no good work or the prospect of getting a good paying job. Doubt makes them disbelieve their own positive dreams and sweep it away as rubbish. They declare such dream impossible. They forget that what it takes to make their positive dreams possible is their faith. Jesus says, "With God all things are possible" (Matthew 19:26) and *"everything is possible for him who believes"* (Mark 9:23). Your positive dreams are possible with God if only you can just believe them and act on them.

King Solomon had a dream. In that dream, he dialogued with God and requested for wisdom from God. In answer to his request, God spoke these words to him in that dream,

I will do what you have asked. I will give you a wise and discerning heart, so that there will never have been anyone like you, nor will there ever be. Moreover, I will give you what you have not asked for–both riches and honour–so that in your lifetime you will have no equal among kings.

1 Kings 3:12-13.

When Solomon awoke, he realized it had been a dream (1 Kings 3:15). Nothing spectacular happened in and after the dream. No laying of hand in the dream. No shaking and nothing unusual happened in the dream.

But he believed God through His words to him in a dream.

Sometime later, he was confronted with a crucial issue involving life and death, the challenge to give a living baby to the true mother. What an enormous challenge! There was no DNA test then and no scientific way to discover the true mother. But Solomon believed his dream. He believed he had wisdom to fathom out mysteries. Without any prayer or any spiritual maneuver, he took the challenge and asked that the baby be divided equally and given to the two women. Is that not madness? What was Solomon up to? Does he want to commit murder? Divide the baby? Solomon, you must be behind yourself!

H-o-l-d on, Solomon is going somewhere. He is up to something. His instruction is a set-up. Oh the true feeling of a mother for her own child cannot be hidden! Emotions speak. Love cries. A mother's compassion can't stand the death of her own child. No sooner than the instruction was given, the true mother spoke, *"Don't kill him! Please, my Lord, give her the living baby!"* (1 Kings 3:26a). Love and compassion forbid killing. Rather they give.

Not so with wickedness and hatred. Hatred is murderous and also speaks. "No" snapped the imposter. She spoke venoms, *"Cut him in two! Neither I nor you shall have him"* (1 Kings 3:26b). What a revelation! What an exposure! Without any DNA test or any other medical, scientific know-how, we can all say, without any iota of doubt, who the true mother is. Instantly, Solomon ruled, *"Give the living baby to the first woman. Do not kill him; she is his mother"* (1 Kings 3:27). By wisdom kings reign and rulers make laws that are just (Proverbs 8:15). Yes, that is wisdom in action. Solomon got it. It was spoken to him in a dream. When he awoke, he believed his dream. And when the challenge came, he acted on his belief.

In a dream, wisdom was imparted to Solomon through speech. He believed it in the physical world. And today, Solomon remains a marvel to all. Believe your dreams. Act on them and dare great things in the physical world.

Your dream can distinguish you. Dream believed is dream acted on. Dream acted on makes the actor a marvel to his or her world (1 Kings 3:28). Startle your world with your dreams.

Your Choice in Dream

In every dream, whether positive or negative, you are left with a choice. This choice includes who you will like to share your dreams with, whether you will like to keep your dreams in mind, and which one you want to keep; who you will like to interpret your dreams: yourself or someone else; how you will like to response to the interpretation of your dreams. And if it is a negative dream, what you will like to do: keep silent over its negative interpretation or refute and rebuke it and apply it to your enemies, or if it calls for a change of lifestyle: will you be willing or not? If it is a positive dream, will you call it impossible or dare to believe it and act on it? Remember, the choice is yours. Every dream unraveled, leaves a person with choices. Make the right ones and profit from your dreams, especially positive ones. Remember, *"Don't despise [dreams], but test all things. Hold on to what is good. Stay away from every form of evil"* (1 Thessalonians 5:20-22 HCSB).

4

Biblical Truths That Dreams Reaffirm

Dream is a world of its own. It is a world of mysteries. Humans dream, and as such participate in this world of mysteries. As a world, dreams are divinely designed to communicate certain truths. These truths are already revealed in the Scripture. Dreams do not affirm and confirm these truths because they are already affirmed and attested to in the Scripture. Dreams only reaffirm these truths in other ways. But most times, people cannot discover the truths by themselves though all humans dream.

I decided to share these truths because these truths, though not contained in one experience of dream, are the unspoken truths underlining every positive or negative dream. These are truths already revealed in the Scripture. But the experience of dream makes their emphases expedient.

1. There is another world beyond this physical one. Some people only believe what they can see with their physical eyes. There are a lot of things we experience in this world that are invisible and abstract but our experiences of these things make them real. Wind, though invisible, can be experienced. The same goes for most chemical gases, for instance, oxygen, carbon dioxide and others that we can only see through scientifically designed instruments. Love is abstract but experiential. Our desires for and experiences of love, though abstract, make love real. We live in a world where we experience several invisible and abstract things. Our experiences without even seeing them confirm their existence and reality.

Dream is experiential. In dreams, a person is exposed to another world. That world has places and is indwelt by persons (some familiar and some strange). In that world the dreamer experiences relationship, dialogue, events and also retains knowledge and consciousness. That world like our physical world is also presented and experienced differently by all dreamers. There is a world out there beyond our physical world where persons live, relate, discuss, interact and things happen, though its happenings are beyond our imagination. It is mysterious to our human minds and senses. Notwithstanding, it is real because we experience it at one time or the other. Dreams tell us most times of another world beyond our physical world. Get the message and find it.

2. *This world is closer to us than imagined.* It took explorers months and years to discover the different continents and nations of the world. Every continent discovered was termed "a new world". Today, it takes hours and sometimes days to fly from one continent (that is, your world) to another. It is another world because the places, peoples and their cultures are different. But it takes just closing our physical eyes for us to step into the world of dream. There we see and meet different places, people and events quite unlike ours. Here events and happenings occur at a speed beyond our human comprehension. When we awake, we know this world is real because our contacts are real.

When we sleep, we dream. Our dream exposes us to this world of mysteries. Mysteries that can and are fathomed by those who care enough to. It may cost you a fortune to travel the world. But it only takes just a slumber or sleep to visit and travel this world of dream. It is the closest world to you than you can imagine. Explore it. Unravel its mysteries.

3. *There are deep mysteries in this world that only a supernatural being (God) can properly account for.* In this world we see things and persons that are mind boggling. We experience events and happenings that are inexplicable. We do things that are beyond our physical abilities and capacities. The fluidity and rapidity with which events happen are dumbfounding. Our world can't fathom it. Our knowledge is stressed beyond limit. No field of human endeavour and discipline has the answer. For instance, how can seven ugly and gaunt cows eat up other seven fat and sleek cows and still remain the same in size and shape (Genesis 41:1-4,17-21)? The same goes for the seven thin and scorched ears of corn and the seven healthy and good ears of corn (Genesis 41:5-7, 22-24)?

Pharaoh's wise men and magicians couldn't explain it (Genesis 41:24). But when Joseph stood before Pharaoh, he declared, *"I cannot do [interprete or explain] it,* **but God will give Pharaoh the answer he desires"** (Genesis 41:16, emphasis mine). The mysteries of dreams tell us there is God. And only God can help a person unravel its mysteries. The mysteries of dreams are meant to show the limitation of man and his knowledge. Some dreams rubbish any known and acceptable formulae of interpreting dreams.

When Nebuchadnezzar placed before his wise men, enchanters, magicians or diviners the unheard of task of telling him his dream and then the interpretation, they replied, *"there is not a man on earth who can do what the king [is asking. The task is too difficult]... No-one can reveal it to the king except the gods, and they do not live among men"* (Daniel 2:10-11). But when

Daniel finally emerged, he declared, *"No wise man, enchanter, magician or diviner can explain to the king the mystery he has asked about,* ***but there is a God in heaven who reveals mysteries.*** *He has shown King Nebuchadnezzar what will happen in days to come"* (Daniel 2:27-28, emphasis mine). Dream is God's designed medium for revealing mysteries. And He only has the true and perfect interpretation of all mysteries. Dreams point us to God as the Creator, Designer and Interpreter of man and his world including dreams.

In the final statement of his interpretation, Daniel again declared, "The great God has shown the king what will take place in the future. The dream is true and the interpretation is trustworthy" (Daniel 2:45b). At this, Nebuchadnezzar fell prostrate before Daniel and paid him honour, declaring, *"Surely your God is the God of gods and the Lord of kings and a revealer of mysteries, for you were able to reveal this mystery"* (Daniel 2:47). May your dreams cause you to worship the one and only true God. He is the only being who can properly account for every mystery in this world of dream. Bow before Him, and accept His love in the person of His Son Jesus Christ (John 3:16).

4. *Only the Bible, not science, has the answers to the mysteries of dreams.* Dream is a world of mysteries, and its mysteries are deeper, higher and wider than our physical world and being can comprehend. Science relates only to things in our physical world and planets. But the Bible alone enlightens us about the world of dreams. Several dreams and their interpretations are documented in the Bible. These records teach us principles and precepts (guidelines) for unraveling dreams' mysteries. This book is based on biblical revelation. Read it. Study it. Meditate on it. Pray to its God. And the mysteries of your dreams will be

unraveled. The Bible will introduce you to a divine teacher, guide and leader who will always ensure your victory in this world of dreams (John 14:26; 16:13; Romans 8:14). The ability to understand dreams displayed in Joseph and Daniel came from Him.

5. Our physical world is controlled by forces beyond the visible. When a person dreams, most times, the dreamer relates with persons and forces beyond the visible. Jacob was first exposed to the God of his fathers, Abraham and Isaac and a host of angelic beings by dream (Genesis 28:12-15). These are invisible beings. Abimelech and Solomon discussed with God in dream (Genesis 20:3-7; 1 Kings 3:5-14). Joseph's interpretation of Pharaoh's dreams showed that God is the one who determines the times and seasons (abundance and famine) of our physical world (Genesis 41:28-32).

Through dreams God reveals that He speaks, warns, restrains (Genesis 20:3-7; 31:24), blesses with wisdom, wealth, fame, honour and long life (1 Kings 3:5-14), encourages (Judges 7:9-15), directs (Matthew 1:20-21;2:12) and overall rules in the affairs of mankind (Daniel 4:10-17,20-26,34-37). He made Joseph's dreams, Pharaoh's, Solomon's, Nebuchadnezzar's, Daniel's and many more come true. Dreams make us know that there is a God who created us and this universe, and that He, not nature or any other thing or being, controls the affairs of the entire universe. He gives and controls dreams and their mysteries. See Him and His fingers in your dreams. With Him, all your positive dreams can come true and all your negative dreams can be averted.

6. Humans are not just physical beings with physical bodies. While our physical bodies are resting and lying down on our beds or wherever asleep, we are exposed to another world, the dream land. In that world of dream, we find ourselves with another body, though like our physical bodies in appearance. This body can do incredible things beyond our physical bodies. This body can scale the walls of a city, run through an army troop, fly over hills, valleys, mountains and any barrier, can ascend and suspend in mid-air, can interact with spirits and other beings and do many more things. Our knowledge in this world is heightened and increased. Our consciousness and sensitiveness are also increased. You are sometimes dressed differently. Your appearance and performance are per excellent.

The question is: "Who is this: the sleeping man or another?" "How comes this person can do and understand things he or she was never trained or taught in the physical?" This obviously, is your spirit man. That is your real you. You are more than a body. You are a spirit being with deeper and higher consciousness than you assume on earth. You have the capacity and potentials to live and operate beyond this physical world. The fact that you never appear bodiless in dreams means you can never appear bodiless in any realm of life. God always has an appropriate body suitable for every realm you enter in life. No wonder Paul called them *"foolish"* that ask, *"How are the dead raised? With what kind of body will they come?"* (1 Corinthians 15:35-38). God is in every realm of life and He already and always has a suitable body designed for whatever realm of life He takes us. Dreams tell us we are more than just physical beings with physical bodies. Let dream give you a foretaste of the world beyond the physical.

7. There is communication beyond the physical in this world. Though asleep in the physical, when we dream we communicate with other beings. Some of these beings are familiar and others are strange. No matter their forms and appearances, in dreams we discus, dialogue and interact with them. In this world, though our physical organs of communication are asleep, when we awake, we can still recall our communication verbatim. We are, most times, fully conscious of who, what and when we met and interacted with. Our communication goes beyond our physical world. In dream we communicate. When we awake, we desire a full understanding of what transpired in our dreams. We want to reveal dreams' mysteries because dreams communicate messages.

Joseph got the message of his dreams and this became his vision for life. He ran with it and saved his family and world. Pharaoh unraveled the message behind the mysteries of his dreams and sprang into action to salvage his kingdom and entire generation. Solomon also received the message of his dream and became a great blessing to the world. You too can unravel the mysteries of dreams when you realize your communication goes beyond the physical in this world. Dream is a medium of communication. Explore it to profit you, your family and your generation.

8. Death is not just physical because its causes are beyond natural. Pharaoh dreamed of seven years of abundance and seven years of famine in one dream. Both happened in the physical world. Nebuchadnezzar dreamed of his banishment from the kingdom for seven years and it came to pass. The decree to banish Nebuchadnezzar was announced by a holy messenger in a dream. The messenger came down from heaven. It was decreed that his mind be changed from that of a man to that of animal (Daniel 4:13-17). The change happened in the physical world. Nebuchadnezzar became an animal and behaved like one (Daniel 4:31-33).

Some deaths are orchestrated in the world of dream. When they happen, their causes are not natural. Dreams tell us life's events are most times orchestrated in another world. Our dreams most times have strong bearings on our existence here in the physical world. Dreams of death should not be treated lightly because the causes of death are beyond the natural. Not all deaths are natural. Remember Pharaoh's chief baker's death (Genesis 40:16-19,22). He dreamed of it before its actual occurrence in the physical world.

9. *Death is not the end of life.* In dreams, some persons, once a while do see and relate with dead individuals, especially relatives and friends. When people do have and hear of such dreams, we should realize that these individuals, even when impersonated, are still alive somewhere beyond the physical world. Some are well dressed, looking good, and bring good messages. God, not only the devil, sometimes uses familiar faces, sometimes dead individuals, to communicate His message to us.

The challenge is being able to discern who the individual was before death in terms of spiritual relationship with God, what role(s) the dead individual fulfill and what kind of message(s) the individual communicate in such dream. Remember, there is no biblically approved formula for interpreting dream. You are the real interpreter and determinant of your dream. So be wise and discerning, and always live and walk in the Spirit. Notwithstanding, through dreams, we can learn that these dead individuals are still alive to God. Death never terminates life. Jesus affirms this in his allusion to Moses' statement at the burning bush and his explication of Moses' statement in Luke 20:37-

38: *"But that the dead are raised, even Moses showed, in the passage about the burning bush, where he calls the Lord the God of Abraham, and the God of Isaac, and the God of Jacob. Now He is not the God of the dead but of the living; **for all live to Him**"* (NASB, emphasis mine). There is certainly life beyond death.

10. *The things of this world appear and appeal differently to different individuals depending on a person's conviction (faith) and relationship to God in Life.* When Nebuchadnezzar dreamed of the kingdoms of this world, he saw a colossal statue beautifully adorned (Daniel 2:31-36). The various metals used to adorn this statue show how beautiful and precious this world and its kingdoms appeared and appealed to Nebuchadnezzar. But when Daniel, God's servant and prophet dreamed of the same kingdoms, he saw frightening and terrifying beasts emerging from the sea. Their appearances were disgusting and disturbing, and their speeches blasphemous. There was nothing in them to desire nor live and die for. But for Nebuchadnezzar, these kingdoms were worth a person's entire life aspiration and pursuit.

The world and its supposed glamour and glory come and go. Nothing in it lasts forever. They are always changing and decaying. Only God's kingdom lives and endures for ever. Nebuchadnezzar went ahead and built a monumental image of himself for all to worship. But Shadrach, Meshach and Abednego messed up his glory and greatness. Let God, through dreams, reveal this world's true worth to you. It is worth nothing and of no lasting value. The world and all that are in it are passing away (1 John 2:15-17).

The true message of Nebuchadnezzar's dream is that every kingdom of this world will be changed and all will be destroyed, replaced and eventually dominated by God's kingdom. Daniel 2:34-35 declares,

while you were watching, a rock was cut out, but not by human hands. It struck the statue on its feet of iron and clay and smashed them. Then the iron, the clay, the bronze, the silver and the gold were broken to pieces at the same time and became like chaff on a threshingfloor in the summer. The wind swept them away without leaving a trace. But the rock that struck the statue became a huge mountain and filled the whole earth.

In his interpretation, Daniel asserted that,

In the time of those kings, the God of heaven will set up a kingdom that will never be destroyed, nor will it be left to another people. It will crush all those kingdoms and bring them to an end, but it will itself endure for ever. This is the meaning of the vision of the rock cut out of a mountain, but not by human hands – a rock that broke the iron, the bronze, the clay, the silver and the gold to pieces.

"The great God has shown the king what will take place in the future. The dream is true and the interpretation is trustworthy."
Daniel 2:44-45-

Nebuchadnezzar missed that message. Every dream points a person to a life and kingdom beyond this world. Seek that life and kingdom. It is real and attainable (Matthew 6:33). Jesus is its king and the way. In John 14:6, Jesus declares, *"I am the way and the truth and the life."*

Conclusion

Dream is a universal experience that cuts across all human barriers. It cuts across nationalities, races, religions, sexes and whatever status of life.

Dream is a world of mysteries. In it, a person is exposed to persons, events, happenings, relationships, dialogues, discussions and interactions beyond our physical world.

Dream affects a person's pneuma-psycho-physiological nature. It is a state one enters when asleep. In it, a person's consciousness and knowledge are fully awake and alert. In dreams, some persons experience bliss, others terror, and still others bizarreness.

When one awakes from this state, a person's consciousness and memory are tasked. Some people do recall completely, others partially and for some others, their memory is blank. They might be conscious that they did dream, but "What exactly?" they cannot fathom. Unfortunately everyone dreams, but not everyone recalls.

When a person recalls his or her dream, the dreamer is faced with the enormous task of interpreting such dream. The interpretation of our dream reveals its type as either positive or negative or empty.

When a dream is empty, it has no substance, no meaning and no interpretation. Empty dreams, most times, spring from much work, busyness, anxiety (worry), and hunger and thirst or overfeeding or late eating and drunkenness.

Positive dreams have positive interpretations and meanings. They engender hope, and inspire promises. They are good and do come to pass. Positive dreams have their source in God and good thoughts.

Negative dreams are evil and negative in interpretations and meanings. They can come to pass if left untackled. They have their source in the devil and his cohorts, and evil thoughts.

A dream has the potential to trouble, frighten, terrify, sadden and also gladden and encourage a person based on the type of dream. A dream can cause a person to be mocked and hated.

Dream is designed by God to warn a person of an impending disaster, to change a person's course of action from evil to good, from wickedness to righteousness, and to suppress a person's pride. Dream as a divine medium of revelation can reveal to a person a glimpse of one's destiny and thus enable such a person to plan and prepare for the future.

All dreams can be adequately tackled. Positive dreams should be stored in a person's mind when properly interpreted either by self or by another. How a dream is interpreted is very dicey. As a result, you must not be silenced over the interpretation of your dreams. Positive dreams should be believed and acted on to ensure its occurrence. This is the only way we can profit from positive dreams and become a blessing to our world.

Negative dreams should be refuted, rebuked and applied to our enemies. Let no one have the final say over your dreams. You are the real interpreter and determinant of your dream and its future. When a dream speaks of changing your way of life, please heed its message and change your lifestyle, especially when you are not living right with God.

Repeated dreams must be noted and tackled appropriately because if left to itself or swept aside, they can occur. In every dream, you are left with a wide range of choices. These include who to share your dreams with, who you will like to have the final say over your dreams, and how you will want such dream to be tackled depending on its nature and source(s).

Dream is divinely designed to communicate to every dreamer certain biblical truths. Dream teaches every dreamer that there is another world beyond our physical world, that that world is closer to us than we can imagine; that there are deep mysteries in that world that only a supernatural being called God can properly account for; that the answers to these mysteries can only be found in the Bible; that our physical world is governed by forces beyond the visible; that human beings are more than just physical bodies; that communication goes beyond the physical in this world; that death and its causes are beyond the natural, and that death by no means implies the end of a person's life. There is life beyond death.

Dream also teaches that the things of this world appear and appeal differently to different individuals depending on their relationship to God. Only God's kingdom is eternal. All who desire to live eternally must bow their knees to God through His Son, Jesus Christ.

Now you can dream meaningfully, explore the world of dreams and unravel its mysteries.

www.ingramcontent.com/pod-product-compliance
Lightning Source LLC
Chambersburg PA
CBHW022121090426
42743CB00008B/946